ⓘⓂ = I LOVE ME

Hello Beautiful people and welcome to your self Love Journal. Firstly, Self Love does not mean "Selfish". Loving yourself more is the first step on many people's healing journey from whatever you have been through or whatever you are currently dealing with.

The purpose of this journal is the help you regain or build that self Love and empowerment on a daily basis. Read the affirmation and attack it from your heart and soul. There is enough space provided for you to be able to come back at a later date and add in more positivity and self Love.

Remember that you deserve all the good things in life, regardless of whatever you may have been conditioned to believe. Now, stop reading and get to Loving yourself!

~ Yours Truly
Lee Hamd
@mentalhealness

How to Use

There is no better time than the present to work on and build up that self Love. So.... Let's get started on how to use this journal.

First, look through the affirmations and decide which one(s) you want to work on. (You can choose more than one!) Once you choose the affirmation, read the definition carefully, absorb it and describe which way that affirmation applies to you. There is no wrong way to do it and YOU get to apply it to yourself, there is no one that can take that away from you. You are validating yourself and you don't need anyone else to do it!

For example - (I'm Enough)

- I am enough just the way I am.
- I am enough for ME and that's what matters to me the most.
- I'm Enough for my family, friends and anyone that I interact with.
- I'm Enough for my children... etc

It's completely up to YOU how you choose to fill it out. Thank you again because You are enough for Me :)

- Lee Hannock

wor·thy (*adjective*) - having or showing the qualities or abilities that merit recognition in a specified way

wor·thy (*adjective*) - having or showing the qualities or abilities that merit recognition in a specified way

e·nough (*adjective*) - Sufficient to meet a need or satisfy a desire

e·nough (*adjective*) - Sufficient to meet a need or satisfy a desire

strong (*adjective*) - having moral or intellectual power / having or marked by great physical power

strong (*adjective*) - having moral or intellectual power / having or marked by great physical power

a·ware (*adjective*) - having a resolute will or morally firm and incorruptible character

a·ware (*adjective*) - having a resolute will or morally firm and incorruptible character

re·sil·ient (*adjective*) - able to withstand or recover quickly from difficult conditions

re·sil·ient (*adjective*) - able to withstand or recover quickly from difficult conditions

good (*adjective*) - possessing or displaying moral virtue.

good (*adjective*) - possessing or displaying moral virtue.

heal·ing (*noun*) - the process of making or becoming sound or healthy again

heal·ing (*noun*) - the process of making or becoming sound or healthy again

learn·ing (*noun*) - the acquisition of knowledge or skills through experience

learn·ing (*noun*) - the acquisition of knowledge or skills through experience

growing (*adjective*) - becoming greater over a period of time; increasing

growing (*adjective*) - becoming greater over a period of time; increasing

grate·ful (*adjective*) - feeling or showing an appreciation of kindness; thankful

grate·ful (*adjective*) - feeling or showing an appreciation of kindness; thankful

pow·er·ful (*adjective*) - having great power or strength.

pow·er·ful (*adjective*) - having great power or strength.

lov·ing (*adjective*) - feeling or showing love or great care.

lov·ing (*adjective*) - feeling or showing love or great care.

thriv·ing (*adjective*) - characterized by success or prosperity

thriv·ing (*adjective*) - characterized by success or prosperity

fear·less (*adjective*) - lacking fear

fear·less (*adjective*) - lacking fear

brave (*adjective*) - ready to face and endure danger or pain; showing courage

brave (*adjective*) - ready to face and endure danger or pain; showing courage

spe·cial (*adjective*) - better, greater, or otherwise different from what is usual

spe·cial (*adjective*) - better, greater, or otherwise different from what is usual

em·pow·ered (*adjective*) - having the knowledge, confidence, means, or ability to do things or make decisions for oneself.

em·pow·ered (*adjective*) - having the knowledge, confidence, means, or ability to do things or make decisions for oneself.

tal·ent·ed (*adjective*) - having a natural aptitude or skill for something.

tal·ent·ed (*adjective*) - having a natural aptitude or skill for something.

loved (*adjective*) - held in deep affection; cherished

loved (*adjective*) - held in deep affection; cherished

ca·pa·ble (*adjective*) - able to achieve efficiently whatever one has to do; competent

ca·pa·ble (*adjective*) - able to achieve efficiently whatever one has to do; competent

un·stop·pa·ble (*adjective*) - impossible to stop or prevent

un·stop·pa·ble (*adjective*) - impossible to stop or prevent

con·fi·dent (*adjective*) - feeling or showing confidence in oneself; self-assured

con·fi·dent (*adjective*) - feeling or showing confidence in oneself; self-assured

vi·tal (*adjective*) - absolutely necessary or important; essential

vi·tal (*adjective*) - absolutely necessary or important; essential

fun (*adjective*) - amusing, entertaining, or enjoyable

fun (*adjective*) - amusing, entertaining, or enjoyable

fo·cus (*verb*) - to concentrate attention or effort

fo·cus (*verb*) - to concentrate attention or effort

proud (*adjective*) - having or showing a high or excessively high opinion of oneself or one's importance

proud (*adjective*) - having or showing a high or excessively high opinion of oneself or one's importance

ex·traor·di·nar·y (adjective) - different in type or greater in degree than the usual or ordinary

ex·traor·di·nar·y (adjective) - different in type or greater in degree than the usual or ordinary

de·serv·ing (*adjective*) - worthy of being treated in a particular way

de·serv·ing (*adjective*) - worthy of being treated in a particular way

free (*adjective*) - not under the control or in the power of another; able to act or be done as one wishes.

free (*adjective*) - not under the control or in the power of another; able to act or be done as one wishes.

con·sist·ent (*adjective*) - acting or done in the same way over time, especially so as to be fair or accurate.

con·sist·ent (*adjective*) - acting or done in the same way over time, especially so as to be fair or accurate.

(Your Choice, make your own affirmation and go with it)

(Your Choice, make your own affirmation and go with it)

(Your Choice, make your own affirmation and go with it)

(Your Choice, make your own affirmation and go with it)

(Your Choice, make your own affirmation and go with it)

(Your Choice, make your own affirmation and go with it)

(Your Choice, make your own affirmation and go with it)

(Your Choice, make your own affirmation and go with it)

(Your Choice, make your own affirmation and go with it)

(Your Choice, make your own affirmation and go with it)

(Your Choice, make your own affirmation and go with it)

(Your Choice, make your own affirmation and go with it)

(Your Choice, make your own affirmation and go with it)

(Your Choice, make your own affirmation and go with it)

(Your Choice, make your own affirmation and go with it)

(Your Choice, make your own affirmation and go with it)

(Your Choice, make your own affirmation and go with it)

(Your Choice, make your own affirmation and go with it)

(Your Choice, make your own affirmation and go with it)

(Your Choice, make your own affirmation and go with it)

(Your Choice, make your own affirmation and go with it)

(Your Choice, make your own affirmation and go with it)

(Your Choice, make your own affirmation and go with it)

(Your Choice, make your own affirmation and go with it)

(Your Choice, make your own affirmation and go with it)

Closing Note From Lee

Thank you so much for purchasing my Self Love Journal and taking a big step into your healing. Healing is a journey, not a destination. You can't catch a plane or Bus to "Healing". You have to walk there and you have to realize that "baby" steps are still steps. Heal at your own pace, and go back and add things into your journal as you progress. Don't just write this stuff down, go out and LIVE it! You're so much stronger than you think you are! I can say that as much as I want but it's up to YOU to believe it. Self Love is so rewarding and empowering. I hope this Journal assisted on your Self Love & Healing Journey.

I created a private video just for the people that have purchased this journal. You can post private comments and inspire someone else. → HTTPS://youtu.be/_ea_oJn6XXY

I Appreciate each and every one of you and I'm forever Grateful. Stay Empowered!

Sincerely,
- Lee Himmael
@mentalhealness

Special Thanks

Thank you so much to everyone that made this journal possible behind the scenes.

To Delaney, Evie, Darius, Jalla, Ben, Nia, Lisa and others. Thank you so much for your help in bringing this to life. I am truly grateful for you all.

Last but not least thank YOU, the user, for purchasing this journal and allowing me to be a part of your healing and self love journey.

Cover - Evie Graves @leaveyourmark.ink
Logo - Darius Cobb @aksiongraphix

You can find me @mentalhealness & www.mentalhealness.net

Made in the USA
Middletown, DE
14 April 2025

74199675R00051